© Pep Mc Stone 2024

I0427198

Dedicated to my

Wife

PROLOGUE

Welcome to "Cut the Crap and Start Selling," a no-nonsense guide that strips away the fluff and gets down to the brass tacks of what selling really is — and what it isn't — in both the B2B and B2C environments.

In these pages, we're not going to sugarcoat the reality of sales or peddle the latest sales fads. Instead, we're going to confront the core of selling in its most pragmatic form. This book is about confronting and solving real sales problems, not just dressing them up in jargon and wishful thinking.

The world of sales is often shrouded in myths and misconceptions. Many believe that to be a successful salesperson, you need to possess a specific set of charismatic traits — the gift of gab, a magnetic personality, or an aggressive, go-getter attitude. While these can be advantageous, they are not the essence of what makes a successful salesperson. Sometimes 'selling-traits' can alienate the client!

Selling, at its core, is about understanding needs, providing solutions, and building relationships based on trust and value. It's about identifying and solving real problems for your customers.

In both B2B and B2C sales environments, the fundamentals of selling remain the same. However, the approach and strategy might differ. In B2B sales, the focus is often on building long-term relationships, understanding complex needs, and navigating through a longer sales cycle. In contrast, B2C sales typically involve quicker transactions with a stronger focus on emotional appeal and immediate benefits.

But irrespective of the environment, the primary goal remains: solving the customer's problem.

This book will guide you through understanding these problems in-depth, adopting a problem-solving mindset, and applying practical strategies to address them effectively. We'll explore how to cut through the noise, focus on what truly matters, and adapt your approach to different selling scenarios.

One of the most critical lessons you'll learn here is the importance of listening and empathy. Sales is not about pushing a product or service; it's about understanding the customer's pain points and offering a solution that makes their life easier or their business more successful. You'll learn how to listen actively, ask the right questions, and tailor your solutions to the customer's unique needs and circumstances.

We will also delve into the significance of continuous learning and adapting to the ever-evolving landscape of sales. The world is changing rapidly, and so are the needs and behaviours of customers. Staying informed about industry trends, new technologies, and changing market dynamics is crucial. This book will equip you with the tools and knowledge to stay ahead of the curve.

Moreover, we'll address the common challenges and obstacles you might face in your sales journey, providing practical advice and strategies to overcome them. Whether it's dealing with rejection, navigating complex sales negotiations, or managing a diverse portfolio of clients, you'll learn how to tackle these challenges head-on and emerge stronger.

"Cut the Crap and Start Selling" is not just a book; it's a reality check and a toolkit for anyone looking to improve their sales skills. Whether you're a seasoned sales veteran or just starting, this book will help you strip away the unnecessary and focus on what really leads to successful selling.

So, buckle up and get ready to embark on a journey to becoming a better, more effective salesperson — one who understands the real problems and knows how to solve them. It's time to cut the crap and start selling.

Pep Mc Stone

1.

NO AUDIENCE, WON'T SELL

In today's dynamic and competitive marketplace, success in sales is not just about having a great product or service. It's about understanding and connecting with your audience in a way that resonates with their needs and aspirations. This requires a deep understanding of who your target market is, what they are looking for, and how your product or service can address their specific pain points.

Why Understanding Audience is Important?

Understanding your audience is crucial for several reasons:

1. **Personalisation:** By understanding your audience, you can tailor your messaging and approach to resonate with them on a personal level. This personalisation not only shows that you care about their needs but also makes them feel like they are getting a more relevant and valuable experience.

2. **Increased Engagement:** When you connect with your audience on an emotional level, you are more

likely to capture their attention and engagement. This can lead to stronger relationships, better communication, and ultimately, more sales.

3.   **Improved Value Proposition:** By understanding your audience's needs and pain points, you can better articulate the value proposition of your product or service. This will help potential customers see how your offering can make a positive impact on their lives.

4.   **Effective Negotiation:** Understanding your audience's mindset can help you anticipate objections and negotiate more effectively. This can lead to more favourable deals and a stronger relationship with the customer.

5.   **Loyalty and Retention:** Building strong relationships with your audience can foster loyalty and encourage repeat business. This will have a significant impact on your bottom line.

How to Understand Your Audience?

To effectively understand your audience, you need to gather information about their demographics, interests, needs, pain points, and buying behaviours. This information can be gathered through a variety of methods, including:

1.   **Market research:** Analyse data from industry reports, surveys, and social media analytics to gain insights into your target market.

2.   **Customer feedback:** Collect feedback through surveys, interviews, and social media interactions to understand what your current and potential customers need and want.

3. **Content analysis:** Analyse the content your audience consumes, such as websites, blogs, and social media posts, to identify their interests and preferences.

4. **Personalised interactions:** Engage with your audience directly through social media, email, or phone calls to get a deeper understanding of their specific needs.

Connecting with Your Audience

Once you have a good understanding of your audience, you can start to connect with them in a meaningful way. This involves building relationships, establishing trust, and demonstrating that you care about their needs. Here are some tips for connecting with your audience:

1. **Focus on empathy:** Put yourself in your audience's shoes and understand their perspectives and challenges.

2. **Show genuine interest:** Take the time to listen to their concerns and ask thoughtful questions.

3. **Be authentic and transparent:** Share your own experiences and insights to build trust and rapport.

4. **Use storytelling:** Engage your audience with relatable stories that illustrate the benefits of your product or service.

5. **Be consistent and proactive:** Maintain regular communication with your audience through social media, email, or other channels.

After connecting with your audience, it's important to keep them engaged and interested. This can be done through a variety of strategies:

1. **Create valuable content:** Provide relevant and informative content that addresses their pain points and interests.

2. **Host interactive events:** Organise webinars, workshops, or online forums to foster community and engagement.

3. **Offer incentives:** Provide discounts, rewards, or exclusive content to encourage participation and loyalty.

4. **Personalise your communication:** Tailor your messaging and offer to specific segments of your audience.

5. **Use social media strategically:** Engage with your audience on social media, respond to comments, and run contests or giveaways.

Understanding, connecting, and engaging with your audience is essential for success in sales. By taking the time to understand their needs, developing personalised relationships, and providing valuable content, you can increase your chances of converting leads into customers and building long-term relationships.

In the dynamic world of sales, the ability to connect with your target market on a deeper level is crucial. This involves understanding their unique needs, aspirations, and pain points, and crafting a sales approach that resonates with their specific context.

The Significance of Identifying Your Target Market

Identifying your target market is the foundation upon which your sales strategy is built. It allows you to focus your efforts on the individuals or businesses that are most likely to value your product or service, thereby maximising your earnings.

By understanding your target market, you gain valuable insights into their:

- **Demographics:** Age, gender, location, income, education, occupation, etc.

- **Psychographics:** Interests, hobbies, lifestyle, values, beliefs, and motivations.

- **Needs:** Specific problems or challenges they are facing that your product or service can address.

- **Pain points:** Frustrations, obstacles, or hindrances that are preventing them from achieving their goals.

- **Buying behaviours:** Preferred communication channels, online habits, decision-making processes, and purchase triggers.

You can achieve this buy building a sales routine or self discipline yourself to start with small talk to identify these key characteristics of you audience or prospects.

Aligning with Target Market Needs: The Key to Effective Sales

When you have a clear understanding of your target market's needs, you can tailor your sales messaging, product offerings, and marketing campaigns to resonate with them directly. This personalised approach not only demonstrates your understanding of their unique challenges but also positions your product or service as the solution they have been seeking.

Harnessing the Power of Data-Driven Insights

In today's data-driven world, sales professionals have access to a wealth of information about their target market. Even if you start from scratch or you face a new walk-in you must read the person's behaviour, looks, dress code, day and time of the day they come in to understand their needs.

Traditionally this data can be collected from various sources, such as:

- **Market research reports:** Insights into industry trends, competitor analysis, and consumer behaviour.

- **Customer feedback:** Surveys, reviews, and interactions with existing or potential customers.

- **Social media analytics:** Insights into online behaviour, interests, and preferences.
- **CRM systems:** Data on past interactions, purchase history, and customer preferences.

By analysing this data, you can identify patterns and trends that reveal deeper customer insights. This data-driven approach can inform your sales strategy, allowing you to optimise your targeting, messaging, and resource allocation.

Understand your Client's Persona

Beyond understanding market data and demographics, effective salesmanship requires the ability to build genuine relationships with potential customers. This involves establishing trust, empathy, and a genuine interest in their needs.

- **Active listening:** Pay attention to their concerns, ask insightful questions, and show genuine interest in their challenges.

- **Storytelling:** Share relevant anecdotes and case studies that illustrate the benefits your product or service has provided to others.

- **Demonstrating expertise:** Share your knowledge and experience in a way that builds confidence and trust.

- **Providing value:** Offer educational resources, helpful tips, and support without pushing for an immediate sale.

By understanding your target market, aligning your offerings with their needs, and building trust-based relationships, you can transform your sales efforts into a powerful engine for growth. This customer-centric approach fosters loyalty, repeat business, and a positive brand reputation, laying the foundation for sustainable success in the ever-evolving sales landscape. Remember, the key to effective selling lies in understanding the people you are trying to reach, their unique needs, and how your product or service can make a significant impact on their lives. By connecting with them on a deeper level, you can unlock the true potential of your sales strategy and achieve remarkable results in the marketplace.

Decoding Customer Needs: Unveiling Pain Points and Motivations for Effective Sales Pitching

In the intricate dance of sales, success often hinges on the ability to understand the customer's perspective, their motivations, and the pain points that drive their purchasing decisions. A sales pitch that resonates with these fundamental aspects transforms from a mere presentation into a compelling narrative that addresses the customer's specific needs and aspirations.

Unearthing the Customer's Pain Points: The Foundation of Effective Pitching

Before crafting a persuasive sales pitch, it's crucial to delve into the underlying pain points that motivate the customer's decision-making process. These pain points could be operational inefficiencies, financial constraints, or unmet business goals. By identifying these pain points, the salesperson can tailor their pitch to address the customer's immediate concerns and demonstrate how their product or service can provide a tangible solution.

Effective pain point identification requires a deep level of empathy and active listening. Salespeople need to step into the customer's shoes, understanding their struggles, frustrations, and the gaps they seek to fill. Active listening, characterised by attentiveness, follow-up questions, and sincere interest, allows the salesperson to uncover the root causes of the customer's pain points.

"WHAT ARE THE BIGGEST CHALLENGES YOU FACE IN ACHIEVING YOUR BUSINESS GOALS?"

Questioning Techniques: Unveiling Hidden Pain Points

A well-structured questioning approach can effectively unveil hidden pain points that may not be apparent on the surface. Open-ended questions, such as "What are the biggest challenges you face in achieving your business goals?" or "What are the areas where you see the most potential for improvement?" can encourage clients to articulate their pain points in detail.

Pain Point Mapping: Visualising the Customer's Challenges

Pain point mapping is a powerful tool to visualise the customer's challenges and their impact on their business operations.By creating a visual representation of the pain points, the salesperson can effectively communicate the severity of the issues and the potential impact of their solution.

Motivational Drivers: Understanding the Customer's Aspirations

While pain points represent the challenges, motivations represent the driving forces that propel the customer towards a solution. Salespeople need to understand the customer's aspirations, their goals, and the desired outcomes they seek to achieve. By aligning their sales pitch with these motivations, the salesperson can tap into the customer's desires and reinforce the value proposition of their offering.

Understanding Business Goals: Connecting with Long-Term Aspirations

Salespeople should delve into the customer's long-term business goals, understanding their vision for growth, expansion, or increased efficiency. By aligning their pitch with these aspirations, they can demonstrate how their solution can contribute to the customer's long-term success and help them achieve their desired outcomes.

Case studies and success stories provide compelling evidence of how the product or service has positively impacted other businesses facing similar challenges. Sharing real-world examples of how the solution has transformed business operations and achieved desired results can resonate with the customer on an emotional level.

A well-crafted sales pitch should be tailored to the specific pain points and motivations of the individual or business being addressed. By highlighting how the product or service can address the customer's unique challenges and align with their aspirations, the salesperson can establish a connection and build trust.

"EFFECTIVE SALES IS NOT JUST ABOUT PITCHING A PRODUCT OR SERVICE; IT'S ABOUT BUILDING RELATIONSHIPS."

Empathetic Dialogue: Beyond Pitching, Building Relationships

Effective sales is not just about pitching a product or service; it's about building relationships. Salespeople should engage in empathetic dialogue, actively listening to the customer's concerns and demonstrating genuine care for their success.This approach fosters trust and credibility, paving the way for a long-lasting partnership.

Pain Point-Driven Pitching: The Path to Customer-Centric Sales

By understanding the customer's pain points and motivations, salespeople can craft persuasive pitches that resonate with their specific needs and aspirations. This customer-centric approach not only enhances the likelihood of closing deals but also fosters long-term relationships and builds a reputation for value-driven selling. Remember, a successful sale is not just about making a transaction; it's about empowering customers to achieve their goals and making a positive impact on their business.

2.
THE ART AND SCIENCE OF ENGAGEMENT

In the world of sales, building rapport and trust with prospective clients is the cornerstone of success. Without these essential foundations, even the most compelling product or service can struggle to gain traction.

This chapter delves into the art of connection, exploring effective strategies for establishing genuine rapport and fostering trust with potential customers for long term success.

The Importance of Rapport and Trust

Rapport and trust are the building blocks of a successful sales relationship. They create a foundation of mutual understanding, respect, and empathy, allowing you to connect with your prospects on a deeper level. When you build rapport and trust with a client, you:

- **Enhance the persuasiveness of your message:** Prospects are more likely to be receptive to your proposals when they feel connected to you and believe that you have their best interests in mind.

23

- **Reduce objections and resistance:** Trustworthy salespeople are seen as credible and knowledgeable, making it easier to address objections and gain buy-in.

- **Strengthen customer relationships:** Rapport and trust foster long-term partnerships, leading to repeat business, referrals, and positive word-of-mouth.

Establishing Common Ground

Building rapport with a prospective client begins by finding common ground, shared interests, or experiences that can serve as a bridge to connect. This can involve:

- **Observing nonverbal cues:** Pay attention to their body language, eye contact, and facial expressions to gauge their interest and level of engagement.

- **Asking open-ended questions:** Engage in active listening, asking questions that encourage them to elaborate on their needs, challenges, and aspirations.

- **Sharing relevant experiences:** Share anecdotes or personal stories that resonate with their situation, demonstrating empathy and understanding.

- **Show genuine interest:** Ask follow-up questions that demonstrate your curiosity and genuine interest in their personal and business or goals.

Active Listening: The Key to Rapport

Active listening is the cornerstone of building rapport and trust. It involves giving your full attention to the prospect, demonstrating empathy and understanding. Here are some active listening techniques you can use:

- **Make eye contact:** Maintain eye contact to show that you are engaged and attentive.

- **Avoid interrupting:** Allow them to finish their thoughts without interjecting.

- **Paraphrase and summarise:** Reiterate what they have said to ensure you understand their perspective accurately.

- **Ask clarifying questions:** Seek additional information to deepen your understanding of their needs and concerns.

Embracing Professionalism and Integrity

Professionalism and integrity are essential qualities in building rapport and trust. These traits are demonstrated through:

- **Being well-prepared:** Research the prospect's company, industry, and challenges to demonstrate your expertise and value. If selling in a B2C environment research typical client challenges.

- **Honesty and transparency:** Be truthful in your communication, avoiding exaggerations or misleading statements - they will back-fire one day.

- **Meeting commitments:** Honour your commitments and keep your promises to build credibility and trust - even small things like returning a call or sending a quote on time helps build micro-trust brownie points.

- **Addressing concerns promptly:** Respond to questions and concerns promptly and professionally.

Building Trust over Time

Building trust with potential clients is an ongoing process that requires consistent effort and attention. Here are some strategies for fostering long-term trust:

- **Follow up regularly:** Maintain regular communication to show your ongoing interest and support.

- **Deliver exceptional service:** Consistently deliver high-quality service and resolve issues promptly.

- **Acknowledge and appreciate feedback:** Value their feedback and use it to improve your offerings.

- **Go the extra mile:** Demonstrate your willingness to go above and beyond their expectations.

The Power of Connection

Building rapport and trust with prospective clients is the foundation of a successful sales career. By connecting with your prospects on a human level, demonstrating empathy, and consistently delivering value, you can establish long-lasting relationships that drive sustainable growth.

Connecting on a Personal Level: Building Professional

Effective communication and relationship building are essential skills for any salesperson. While technical expertise and product knowledge are crucial, they alone cannot guarantee success. To truly connect with your audience on a personal level, you need to establish a professional rapport that transcends mere transactions. This chapter explores the art of building trust and building meaningful relationships with your clients.

The Power of Personal Connection

In today's competitive sales landscape, personal connection is more important than ever. Customers are increasingly seeking not just products or services but also personalised experiences and genuine human engagement. By connecting with your audience on a personal level, you can:

Enhance understanding: Deeper connections foster a better understanding of your client's needs, challenges, and aspirations.

Build trust: Personalised interactions and genuine interest create a foundation of trust that makes it easier to close deals.

Nurture loyalty: Establishing personal relationships fosters customer loyalty and encourages repeat business.

Create advocates: Satisfied customers become brand advocates, spreading positive word-of-mouth and attracting new prospects.

Key Strategies for Personal Connection

Building personal connection in sales requires a holistic approach that encompasses not just verbal communication but also nonverbal cues, active listening, and empathy. Here are some key strategies to consider:

Show genuine interest: Demonstrate genuine enthusiasm for your client's business and their goals.

Ask thoughtful questions: Engage in active listening by asking questions that go beyond surface-level inquiries.

Reflect their emotions: Acknowledge and validate their feelings, demonstrating empathy and understanding.

Share relevant stories: Personal anecdotes can resonate with your client and create a sense of connection.

Embrace Cultural Sensitivity

Cultural sensitivity plays a vital role in building personal connections. Respecting cultural differences and adapting your communication style can make a significant impact:

Research cultural norms: Understand the cultural context and etiquette to avoid missteps or offence.

Be mindful of language: Use language appropriate to the culture and avoid cultural stereotypes or assumptions.

Be respectful of traditions: Respect local customs and avoid imposing your own cultural values.

Utilise Technology for Connection

Technology can be a powerful tool for enhancing personal connection, but it's essential to use it judiciously:

Personalise emails: Use personalisation tools to address your client by name and tailor the message to their interests.

Leverage video conferencing: Video calls can provide a more personal touch, allowing for better visual cues.

Utilize social media platforms: Engage with your clients on social media platforms to build rapport and stay connected.

Overcoming Challenges

Building personal connections in sales can sometimes be challenging, especially when dealing with time constraints or complex sales cycles. Here are some tips for overcoming these hurdles:

Prioritise quality over quantity: Schedule fewer, more focused interactions to allow for deeper connections.

Be patient and persistent: Building rapport takes time and effort. Don't give up if you don't see immediate results.

Continuously improve your communication skills: Practice active listening, empathy, and storytelling to enhance your interactions.

The Long-Term Value of Personal Connection

The value of personal connection in sales extends well beyond the immediate sale. It creates a foundation for long-term partnerships, repeat business, and referrals. By building trust and fostering genuine relationships, you can establish yourself as a trusted advisor and partner, driving sustainable growth for your business.

Demonstrating Genuine Interest and Building Credibility in Sales

Success often hinges on the ability to connect with clients on an emotional level, demonstrating genuine interest in their concerns and goals. This empathy, coupled with a deep understanding of their industry and business challenges, fosters trust and builds credibility, transforming you into a trusted advisor rather than just a sales representative.

The Significance of Empathy in Sales

Empathy is the ability to understand and share the feelings of another person. In the context of sales, empathy allows you to connect with your clients on a deeper level, understanding their motivations, pain points, and aspirations. This emotional connection is crucial for building trust and rapport, which are essential for closing deals and fostering long-term relationships.

Demonstrating Genuine Interest in B2B Sales

In B2B sales, where relationships often span multiple decision-makers, demonstrating genuine interest is paramount. This involves actively listening to their concerns, asking insightful questions, and showing genuine curiosity about their business challenges and goals. By understanding their unique context, you can tailor your solutions and messaging to address their specific needs.

Building Credibility Through Expertise in B2B Sales

Credibility is a key factor in B2B sales. To establish yourself as a trusted advisor, you need to demonstrate your expertise in your industry and your knowledge of their specific business challenges. This can be achieved through:

- **Staying up-to-date on industry trends and developments:** Actively seek out relevant information and insights to demonstrate your knowledge and thought leadership.

- **Sharing case studies and success stories:** Provide concrete examples of how your solutions have helped other businesses achieve their goals.

- **Engaging in thought leadership initiatives:** Write articles, blog posts, or participate in industry events to position yourself as an expert in your field.

Demonstrating Genuine Interest in B2C Sales

In B2C sales, where the focus is often on building emotional connections, demonstrating genuine interest is equally important. This involves understanding their personal motivations, aspirations, and pain points related to the product or service you are offering. By showing genuine care for their well-being, you can build trust and encourage them to make a buying decision.

Building Credibility Through Storytelling in B2C Sales

Storytelling is a powerful tool for building credibility in B2C sales. By sharing relatable stories about how your product or service has positively impacted other customers, you can connect with their emotions and demonstrate the tangible value you can offer.

Harnessing the Power of Technology for Empathy and Credibility

Technology can be leveraged to enhance the empathy and credibility you demonstrate in B2B and B2C sales. Here are some examples:

- **Data-driven insights:** Analyse customer data to identify their pain points, preferences, and purchase patterns.

- **Social media monitoring:** Stay informed about industry trends, customer feedback, and competitor activities.

- **Personalised customer experiences:** Use technology to personalise interactions, offers, and product recommendations.

Overcoming Challenges in Demonstrating Empathy and Credibility

Salespeople often face challenges in demonstrating empathy and credibility, such as:

- **Time constraints:** In fast-paced sales cycles, it can be difficult to engage in deep, empathetic conversations.

- **Objections and resistance:** Dealing with objections can make it challenging to maintain a supportive and empathetic approach.

- **Building trust across multiple decision-makers:** In B2B sales, it's crucial to build trust with multiple stakeholders, which can be time-consuming.

To overcome these challenges, focus on the long-term value of building genuine relationships. Take time to understand each customer's unique needs and address their concerns proactively. By consistently demonstrating empathy and expertise, you can establish yourself as a trusted advisor and drive sustainable sales success.

The Power of Genuine Interest and Credibility in Sales

Demonstrating genuine interest in your clients' concerns and goals is not just a courtesy; it's the foundation for building trust, credibility, and lasting relationships. By actively listening, sharing knowledge, and storytelling, you can position yourself as a trusted advisor and partner, leading to increased sales, customer loyalty, and a positive brand reputation. Remember, empathy is not just about listening; it's about understanding, connecting, and demonstrating that you genuinely care about your customers' success.

3.

COMMUNICATE OR DIE

Effective communication is the cornerstone of success in any sales endeavour. It's the medium through which you connect with potential customers, build relationships, and ultimately, close deals. When you communicate effectively, you can:

- **Position yourself as a trusted advisor:** By demonstrating your knowledge and expertise through clear and concise language, you can establish yourself as a go-to resource for your clients.

- **Build rapport and trust:** Active listening, empathy, and storytelling techniques can foster meaningful connections with your audience, enhancing trust and credibility.

- **Address objections and concerns:** By listening attentively and responding thoughtfully to questions and feedback, you can address objections and overcome sales hurdles.

The Power of Clear and Concise Language

Clarity and conciseness are essential elements of effective communication in sales. Using simple, jargon-free language ensures that your message is easily understood by your audience, regardless of their background or technical expertise.

- **Avoid technical jargon:** Jargon can alienate potential customers, making it difficult for them to grasp the value proposition of your product or service.

- **Use simple, direct language:** Employ everyday language that is easy for your audience to understand. Avoid overly complex sentences or convoluted phrasing.

- **Explain key concepts:** If your product or service involves complex concepts, break them down into smaller, more digestible chunks. Use visuals and analogies to enhance comprehension.

Active Listening: The Art of Understanding

Active listening is a critical skill in sales, allowing you to truly understand your clients' needs, challenges, and aspirations.By actively listening, you can demonstrate empathy, build rapport, and tailor your message accordingly.

- **Pay attention to verbal and nonverbal cues:** Observe body language, facial expressions, and tone of voice to gauge your client's engagement and interest.

- **Ask open-ended questions:** Encourage your client to elaborate on their needs and concerns by asking open-ended questions that go beyond simple "yes" or "no" answers.

- **Summarise and paraphrase:** Rephrase what your client has said to ensure you have accurately understood their message.

Storytelling: Engaging with Emotion

Storytelling is a powerful tool to capture attention, evoke emotions, and connect with your audience on a deeper level. By weaving anecdotes, case studies, and metaphors into your sales conversation, you can:

- **Personalise the message:** Make your message more relatable and memorable by incorporating personal stories and experiences.

- **Demonstrate empathy and understanding:** Share stories that highlight your understanding of your client's challenges and aspirations.

- **Build credibility and expertise:** Showcase your knowledge and experience by sharing relatable case studies and success stories.

Harnessing Technology for Effective Communication

Technology can play a valuable role in enhancing your communication skills and effectiveness in sales. Here are some examples:

- **Communication platforms:** Utilise tools like video conferencing and messaging platforms to foster real-time interactions with your audience.

- **Data analytics:** Analyse sales data to identify patterns and trends in customer interactions, enabling you to tailor your messaging accordingly.

- **Sales enablement tools:** Leverage tools that provide sales teams with access to product information, customer insights, and sales training materials.

"REMEMBER, COMMUNICATION IS NOT JUST ABOUT TRANSMITTING INFORMATION; IT'S ABOUT FORMING MEANINGFUL CONNECTIONS, BUILDING RAPPORT, AND FOSTERING LONG-TERM RELATIONSHIPS THAT DRIVE GROWTH AND PROSPERITY."

Overcoming Communication Challenges

Effective communication in sales can sometimes be challenging. Here are some tips for overcoming common obstacles:

- **Manage time effectively:** Minimise distractions and prioritise your communication efforts to ensure you are fully present and engaged.

- **Address cultural differences:** Adapt your communication style and language to accommodate cultural sensitivities and preferences.

- **Embrace feedback:** Seek feedback from colleagues and mentors to identify areas for improvement and refine your communication approach.

Mastering the Art of Communication

Effective communication is an essential skill for any salesperson. By employing clear and concise language, actively listening, utilising storytelling techniques, and leveraging technology, you can connect with your audience, build trust, and ultimately, achieve sales success. Remember, communication is not just about transmitting information; it's about forming meaningful connections, building rapport, and fostering long-term relationships that drive growth and prosperity.

4.
VALUE PROPOSITION AND SELLING BENEFITS

A strong value proposition serves as the cornerstone of success. It's the compelling message that clearly articulates the unique benefits your product or service offers, differentiating you from the competition and resonating with your target audience. A well-defined value proposition not only attracts potential customers but also guides your sales strategy, ensuring that your messaging is focused and persuasive.

The Essence of a Value Proposition

A value proposition is a concise statement that summarises the key benefits and advantages your product or service provides to your target audience. It answers the question, "Why should customers choose you over your competitors?" A compelling value proposition should:

- **Be clear and concise:** Articulate the value proposition in simple, straightforward language that is easy to understand and remember.

- **Be unique:** Highlight the unique features and benefits that set your product or service apart from others in the market.

- **Be relevant to the customer's needs:** Address the specific pain points and aspirations of your target audience.

- **Be quantifiable:** Whenever possible, quantify the benefits to provide tangible evidence of the value you offer.

Articulating the Unique Value

To craft a powerful value proposition, you need to delve into the core of your product or service, identifying the unique features and benefits that differentiate you from competitors. Consider the following aspects:

- **Problem-solving ability:** How does your offering address the pain points and challenges faced by your target audience?

- **Pain-relieving outcomes:** What specific benefits does your product or service provide to alleviate the pain points of your customers?

- **Value creation:** How does your offering add value to your customers' lives or businesses?

- **Differentiating factors:** What unique features or benefits set your product or service apart from competitors?

- **Competitive advantage:** How does your value proposition position you as the preferred choice among your target audience?

Highlighting Benefits that Matter

The most effective value propositions resonate with the specific needs and aspirations of your target audience. To identify these key benefits, consider their:

- **Pain points:** What are the challenges and frustrations they face that your offering can resolve?

- **Goals and aspirations:** What are their desired outcomes, objectives, or aspirations that your product or service can support?

- **Needs and preferences:** What are their specific requirements, preferences, and priorities when making purchasing decisions?

- **Budget considerations:** What are their price expectations and willingness to pay for the value you offer?

Quantifying the Value Proposition

Quantifying the value proposition adds credibility and impact, demonstrating the tangible benefits your offering provides. Consider using metrics, data, or case studies to showcase:

- **Measurable improvements:** How has your product or service helped customers achieve quantifiable improvements in their business or personal lives?

- **Cost savings:** What are the specific cost savings or ROI that customers can achieve by using your offering?

- **Increased productivity:** How has your product or service improved customer efficiency, productivity, or output?

- **Enhanced customer satisfaction:** What percentage of customers have expressed satisfaction or loyalty after using your offering?

A well-defined value proposition is the cornerstone of effective sales communication. It provides the foundation for crafting compelling marketing messages, engaging sales pitches, and building lasting customer relationships. By articulating the unique benefits you offer, addressing customer needs, and quantifying the value your product or service provides, you can differentiate yourself from competitors, attract more customers, and achieve sustainable sales success. Remember, a value proposition is not just a statement; it's a promise to deliver tangible results that make a positive impact on your target audience.

"A VALUE PROPOSITION IS NOT JUST A STATEMENT; IT'S A PROMISE TO DELIVER TANGIBLE RESULTS THAT MAKE A POSITIVE IMPACT ON YOUR TARGET AUDIENCE."

5.
OVERCOMING OBJECTIONS AND HANDLING CHALLENGES

Objections are an inevitable part of the process. Whether it's concerns about price, features, or compatibility, potential customers often raise objections that can derail the sales journey. However, these objections, when handled effectively, can be transformed into opportunities to strengthen your sales pitch, demonstrate the value of your offering, and ultimately secure the deal.

Anticipating and Preparing for Objections

A skilled salesperson anticipates potential objections and prepares effective responses beforehand. This proactive approach is crucial for maintaining control of the sales conversation and steering it towards a positive outcome. Here are some strategies for anticipating objections:

- **Understand your target audience:** Thoroughly research your target audience, identifying their common pain points, concerns, and decision-making processes. This knowledge will help you anticipate potential objections and tailor your responses accordingly.

- **Analyse sales data:** Review past sales interactions and identify recurring objections that customers have raised.This pattern recognition will help you anticipate and prepare for similar objections in future sales conversations.

- **Seek feedback from colleagues:** Consult with experienced colleagues or mentors to gain insights into common objections and effective rebuttals. Their experience can provide invaluable guidance.

Addressing Objections Proactively and Calmly

When an objection arises, don't be thrown off guard. Instead, approach it as an opportunity to further demonstrate your expertise and the value of your offering. Here are effective strategies for addressing objections proactively and calmly:

- **Acknowledge the objection:** Validate the customer's concern by acknowledging their perspective. This shows empathy and demonstrates your understanding of their needs.

- **Paraphrase the objection:** Repeat the objection back to the customer in your own words. This confirms your understanding and ensures you are addressing the issue accurately.

- **Address the root cause:** Delve deeper into the underlying reason behind the objection. This will help you pinpoint the real concern and address it effectively.

- **Reframe the objection:** Frame the objection as an opportunity to showcase the benefits of your product or service. Explain how your offering can address the customer's concerns and provide value.

"OBJECTIONS ARE NOT ROADBLOCKS; THEY ARE OPPORTUNITIES TO SHOWCASE THE VALUE YOU BRING TO THE TABLE AND ESTABLISH YOURSELF AS A TRUSTED ADVISOR."

Reframing Objections as Opportunities

Instead of viewing objections as obstacles, experienced salespeople recognise them as opportunities to further enhance their sales pitch and highlight the value of their offering. Here are some ways to reframe objections and turn them into advantages:

- **Address price objections:** Emphasise the long-term value and ROI that your product or service can deliver.Explain how the perceived cost is outweighed by the benefits it will bring.

- **Address feature objections:** Demonstrate how your product or service addresses the customer's specific needs and exceeds their expectations. Highlight unique features and benefits that differentiate your offering.

- **Address compatibility objections:** Provide real-world examples of how your product or service has seamlessly integrated with other systems and technologies. Assure the customer that compatibility is not an issue.

Conquering Challenges and Embracing Objections

While objections may initially appear as barriers, they can be transformed into powerful tools for enhancing your sales performance. By anticipating, addressing, and reframing objections effectively, you can demonstrate your expertise, build trust with potential customers, and ultimately secure more deals. Remember, objections are not roadblocks; they are opportunities to showcase the value you bring to the table and establish yourself as a trusted advisor. Embrace the challenges, navigate the objections confidently, and you will undoubtedly pave the way for greater success in your sales endeavours.

6.

NEGOTIATION AND CLOSING THE DEAL

The ability to negotiate effectively and close deals is paramount. It's a dynamic process that requires a deep understanding of human psychology, communication, and strategic thinking. Here we will delve into the critical aspects of negotiation and closing the deal.

The three key strategies essential for closing a negotiated deal can be considered as follows:

1. Setting Clear Expectations and Boundaries during the Negotiation Process

2. Actively Listening to the Buyer's Position and Negotiating Effectively

3. Creating a Sense of Urgency and Encouraging the Buyer to Make a Decision

By mastering these strategies, professional salespeople can not only improve their negotiation skills but also significantly enhance their closing rates, resulting in increased revenue and success.

Negotiation in professional selling is a delicate balance between the salesperson and the buyer. It's crucial to establish a strong foundation by setting clear expectations and boundaries from the outset.

Preparing for Negotiation

1. Define Your Objectives: The negotiation process should always begin with a clear understanding of your objectives. What do you aim to achieve? What is the desired outcome? These questions should guide your negotiation strategy.

2. Thorough Research: Prior to entering negotiations, it's essential to research the buyer, their organisation, and their industry. This knowledge will empower you with insights that can be leveraged during the negotiation.

3. Establishing a BATNA: Your Best Alternative to a Negotiated Agreement (BATNA) is your safety net. Knowing your BATNA ensures you don't accept terms that are less favourable than your alternatives.

Communicating Expectations and Boundaries

1. Clear and Transparent Communication: Effective negotiation begins with open and honest communication. Both parties must articulate their expectations, requirements, and boundaries early in the process to prevent misunderstandings.

2. Setting Ground Rules: Establishing ground rules can provide structure to the negotiation. Ground rules might

include specifying timeframes, confidentiality agreements, and the process for resolving disputes.

3. Building Trust: Trust is the cornerstone of any successful negotiation. Professional salespeople should strive to build trust through transparency, integrity, and a focus on creating value for the buyer.

Managing Expectations Throughout the Process

1. Flexibility: While it's vital to set boundaries, flexibility is equally important. Negotiations often require compromise, and being adaptable when necessary can lead to mutually beneficial agreements.

2. Periodic Check-Ins: Regularly checking in with the buyer throughout the negotiation process ensures that both parties remain aligned and that expectations are being met.

Actively Listening to the Buyer's Position and Negotiating Effectively

Active listening is a skill that professional salespeople should master. It enables them to understand the buyer's perspective and tailor their negotiation strategy accordingly.

The Art of Active Listening

1. Understanding Needs: Active listening involves not just hearing but truly comprehending what the buyer is conveying. Paying close attention to verbal and non-verbal cues helps identify their needs, concerns, and motivations.

2. Empathy: Empathising with the buyer's position builds rapport and trust. It demonstrates that you genuinely care

about their needs and are willing to work together to find a mutually beneficial solution.

3. Asking Clarifying Questions: Open-ended questions and requests for clarification allow you to delve deeper into the buyer's perspective. They also demonstrate your commitment to finding the best solution for them.

Effective Negotiation Techniques

1. Win-Win Approach: In professional selling, the focus should always be on achieving a win-win outcome. This approach emphasises collaborative problem-solving and value creation for both parties.

2. Creating Value: Salespeople can create value by identifying opportunities or concessions that hold little cost for them but significant value for the buyer. This demonstrates a commitment to meeting the buyer's needs.

3. Framing and Anchoring: The way you present your arguments and proposals can significantly impact the perceived value. Techniques like framing and anchoring allow you to strategically shape the negotiation's direction.

Creating a Sense of Urgency and Encouraging the Buyer to Make a Decision

Closing the deal is often the most critical aspect of professional selling. It requires the salesperson to create a sense of urgency and motivate the buyer to commit.

Understanding the Buyer's Decision-Making Process

1. Identifying Decision Makers: In complex sales, identifying and engaging with key decision-makers is

paramount. Focusing your efforts on those who hold the authority expedites the decision-making process.

2. Recognising Decision Triggers: Every buyer has triggers that motivate them to make a decision. These may include financial incentives, competitive pressures, or deadlines. Recognising and leveraging these triggers is essential.

Techniques to Encourage a Decision

1. Limited-Time Offers: Time-sensitive offers, discounts, or incentives can create a sense of urgency. However, it's critical to use these tactics ethically and transparently to maintain trust.

2. Overcoming Objections: Addressing the buyer's concerns and objections promptly can remove barriers to decision-making. Highlight how your proposal addresses their needs and mitigates potential risks.

3. Closing Questions: Using well-crafted closing questions guides the conversation toward a decision. Questions like "Are you ready to move forward?" or "Can we finalise the agreement today?" prompt the buyer to make a commitment.

"MASTERING THE ART OF NEGOTIATION AND CLOSING THE DEAL IS ESSENTIAL FOR SUCCESS IN PROFESSIONAL SELLING."

Mastering the art of negotiation and closing the deal is essential for success in professional selling. By setting clear expectations and boundaries, actively listening and negotiating effectively, and creating a sense of urgency, salespeople can significantly enhance their ability to close deals successfully.

In the competitive world of sales, those who excel in these areas not only secure more business but also build long-lasting relationships with clients. Ultimately, the art of negotiation and closing the deal is a dynamic process that requires continuous improvement and adaptation to the ever-changing landscape of professional selling. When executed with skill and finesse, it can be the key to achieving exceptional results and driving business growth.

7.
RELATIONSHIPS AND LOYALTY

Success is not just about closing deals; it's about building lasting relationships with customers. Today, more than ever, the modern salesperson understands that going beyond the transaction is essential for nurturing long-term customer relationships. Exceptional customer service and support are key drivers in achieving this goal, and offering well-crafted loyalty programs and incentives plays a pivotal role in encouraging repeat business. In this essay, we will explore the significance of these strategies for salespeople and how they can be leveraged to build strong customer relationships and secure long-term success.

Going Beyond the Transaction: The Heart of Sales

A. Understanding the Customer's World

1. Empathetic Selling: Successful salespeople recognise that understanding the customer's needs and challenges goes beyond just knowing their products. They practice empathetic selling by putting themselves in the customer's shoes.

2. Building Trust: Trust is the foundation of any lasting relationship. Salespeople must be transparent, reliable, and honest in their dealings to earn and maintain the customer's trust.

B. Tailoring Solutions to Customer Needs

1. Needs Assessment: Effective salespeople take the time to conduct thorough needs assessments. This involves asking probing questions and actively listening to uncover the customer's pain points and goals.

2. Customisation: Tailoring solutions to meet individual customer needs demonstrates a commitment to their success and fosters loyalty.

C. Communication Skills

1. Active Listening: Sales professionals excel at active listening, allowing them to grasp the nuances of the customer's requirements and concerns.

2. Effective Storytelling: Storytelling is a powerful tool for salespeople to convey the value of their products or services in a relatable and memorable way.

Providing Exceptional Customer Service and Support

Exceptional customer service is the linchpin of building and maintaining customer loyalty. Salespeople play a crucial role in delivering this high level of service.

A. Responsiveness

1. Prompt Communication: Responding to customer inquiries promptly shows respect for their time and needs.

2. Problem Resolution: Salespeople should be adept at resolving customer issues efficiently, often serving as the first line of support.

B. Knowledge and Expertise

1. Product Knowledge: Deep product knowledge allows salespeople to answer questions, make recommendations, and guide customers effectively.

2. Industry Expertise: A salesperson who understands the broader industry context can provide valuable insights and solutions.

C. Post-Sale Support

1. Relationship Continuation: Successful salespeople don't consider the deal done after the sale is closed. They continue to provide support, ensuring the customer's ongoing success.

2. Upselling and Cross-selling: Offering complementary products or services can enhance the customer's experience and value.

Offering Loyalty Programs and Incentives: A Salesperson's Arsenal

Loyalty programs and incentives are potent tools for salespeople to leverage in their efforts to encourage repeat business and foster customer loyalty.

A. Building Loyalty through Rewards

1. Tailoring Incentives: Salespeople can work with their customers to create personalised loyalty programs that align with the customer's preferences and goals.

2. Exclusive Access: Offering loyal customers exclusive access to new products, discounts, or events can make them feel valued and appreciated.

B. Increasing Sales through Incentives

1. Upsell and Cross-Sell Incentives: Salespeople can use incentives to encourage customers to explore additional products or services.

2. Referral Programs: Satisfied customers can become brand advocates by referring new business, and incentives can motivate them to do so.

C. Data-Driven Sales

1. Leveraging Customer Data: Salespeople can use customer data to tailor loyalty programs and incentives effectively.

2. Predictive Analytics: By employing predictive analytics, salespeople can anticipate customer needs and proactively offer relevant incentives.

The Role of Salespeople in Building Customer Relationships and Loyalty

A. Customer Advocates

1. Building Rapport: Salespeople have the opportunity to forge strong personal connections with customers, becoming advocates for the brand.

2. Trustworthy Advisors: Salespeople who consistently provide valuable solutions and exceptional service become trusted advisors to their customers.

B. Driving Customer-Centric Culture

1. Feedback Loops: Salespeople are often the first to hear customer feedback and can play a crucial role in relaying it to the organisation for continuous improvement.

2. Alignment with Customer Goals: Sales professionals align their efforts with the customer's success, making them integral to a customer-centric culture.

C. Leveraging Technology

1. CRM Systems: Customer Relationship Management (CRM) systems empower salespeople to manage relationships, track customer interactions, and deliver personalised experiences.

2. Data Analytics: Utilising data analytics tools, salespeople can gain insights into customer behaviour and preferences, enabling them to tailor their approach effectively.

Challenges and Pitfalls

While building customer relationships and loyalty is crucial for salespeople, they must also be aware of potential challenges and pitfalls that can hinder their efforts.

A. Balancing Short-Term Goals and Long-Term Relationships: Salespeople often face pressure to meet short-term sales targets, which can sometimes conflict with the goal of nurturing long-term customer relationships.

B. Data Privacy and Ethics: The responsible use of customer data and respecting privacy concerns are essential to maintaining trust.

C. Competition: In a competitive marketplace, salespeople must continually innovate and differentiate themselves to secure customer loyalty.

"THROUGH EMPATHY, EXPERTISE, AND THE SKILFUL USE OF TECHNOLOGY, SALESPEOPLE CAN BECOME TRUSTED ADVISORS AND ADVOCATES FOR THEIR CUSTOMERS, ULTIMATELY SECURING A LASTING AND MUTUALLY BENEFICIAL PARTNERSHIP."

In the sales landscape, success hinges on more than just closing deals; it relies on building and nurturing customer relationships and loyalty. Salespeople who understand the importance of going beyond the transaction, providing exceptional customer service and support, and leveraging loyalty programs and incentives are well-positioned for long-term success. These strategies are not only effective but also essential for sales professionals to thrive in an evolving business environment. Through empathy, expertise, and the skilful use of technology, salespeople can become trusted advisors and advocates for their customers, ultimately securing a lasting and mutually beneficial partnership. The challenges are real, but the rewards of building customer relationships and loyalty are immeasurable, making it an essential focus for every salesperson.

8.

ETHICAL SELLING TODAY

E thics serve as the moral compass that guides a salesperson's actions and decisions. Ethical selling practices are not just a matter of compliance or reputation; they are fundamental to establishing trust and building long-lasting customer relationships. The relevance and importance of ethical selling practices for salespeople, focusing on upholding ethical principles, respecting the customer's decisions, and building a reputation for honesty and integrity are important to build a charismatic persona. By examining the impact of ethical behaviour in sales, we can better appreciate its role in today's competitive business landscape.

Upholding Ethical Principles in Sales

A. The Ethics Paradox

1. Ethical Dilemmas in Sales: Sales professionals often encounter situations where ethical dilemmas arise, such as pressure to meet targets, competition, or the temptation to use deceptive tactics.

2. The Relevance of Ethics: Upholding ethical principles in sales is not only morally right but also a practical necessity for long-term success.

B. Avoiding Deceptive Sales Tactics

1. Honesty in Product Representation: Ethical salespeople accurately represent their products or services, avoiding exaggerations or false claims to secure a sale.

2. Transparency in Pricing: Clear and transparent pricing is essential to build trust. Hidden fees or undisclosed charges erode trust and tarnish a salesperson's reputation.

C. Ethical Selling Techniques

1. Consultative Selling: A consultative approach, focused on identifying customer needs and providing tailored solutions, aligns with ethical principles and builds trust.

2. Relationship Building: Building genuine relationships with customers, rather than viewing them as mere transactions, is at the core of ethical selling.

Respecting the Customer's Decision

A. Autonomy and Respect

1. Customer Autonomy: Ethical salespeople respect the customer's right to make independent decisions about their purchases, even if it means not making a sale.

2. Avoiding Pressure: Ethical salespeople refrain from using undue pressure tactics, respecting the customer's pace and preferences.

B. The Long-Term Perspective

1. Customer-Centric Focus: Ethical salespeople prioritise the customer's needs and long-term satisfaction over short-term gains.

2. Repeat Business: Respecting a customer's decision not to buy today can lead to future opportunities and referrals.

Building a Reputation for Honesty and Integrity

A. Trust as the Currency of Sales

1. The Role of Trust: Trust is the cornerstone of sales success. Ethical salespeople understand that their reputation for honesty and integrity directly impacts their ability to build trust with customers.

2. Trustworthiness: Being perceived as trustworthy enhances a salesperson's credibility and makes customers more willing to engage in business.

B. The Impact of Ethical Reputation

1. Positive Word-of-Mouth: Customers who have positive experiences with ethical salespeople are more likely to share their experiences with friends and family, leading to referrals.

2. Repeat Business: Ethical salespeople who consistently deliver on their promises are more likely to secure repeat business from satisfied customers.

C. Ethical Role Models

1. Leadership in Sales Organisations: Ethical salespeople can serve as role models and influence the ethical culture within their organisations, promoting integrity throughout the sales team.

2. The Ripple Effect: Ethical behaviour can inspire others within the industry to prioritise honesty and integrity in their sales practices.

The Relevance of Ethical Selling in Today's Business Landscape

A. The Impact of Social Media

1. Transparency: In the age of social media, customers can easily share their experiences, both positive and negative. Ethical behaviour is vital to avoid public backlash.

2. Online Reputation Management: Ethical salespeople understand the importance of maintaining a positive online reputation to attract and retain customers.

B. The Shift Towards Relationship-Based Selling

1. Relationship-Centric Sales: Modern salesmanship is increasingly moving towards relationship-based selling, emphasising trust, and long-term customer relationships.

2. Differentiation: Ethical sales practices can differentiate a salesperson or organisation in a crowded and competitive marketplace.

C. Ethical Selling and Legal Compliance

1. Compliance with Regulations: Ethical selling practices often align with legal requirements and regulations, reducing the risk of legal consequences.

2. Avoiding Scandals: Ethical behaviour minimises the likelihood of being involved in scandals or controversies that can damage an individual's or organisation's reputation.

Challenges and Pitfalls in Ethical Selling

While ethical selling practices are crucial, salespeople must also be aware of potential challenges and pitfalls they may encounter.

A. Pressure to Achieve Targets: Sales targets can create pressure to resort to unethical tactics to meet quotas. Ethical salespeople must resist this pressure.

B. Ethical Grey Areas: Some situations may present ethical grey areas, where the right course of action is not immediately clear. Ethical salespeople must navigate these challenges with integrity. These are most delicate in a B2C environment.

C. Maintaining Ethical Standards: Consistently upholding ethical principles can be challenging, and salespeople must remain vigilant to avoid lapses in judgment.

" UPHOLDING ETHICAL PRINCIPLES, RESPECTING THE CUSTOMER'S DECISIONS, AND BUILDING A REPUTATION FOR HONESTY AND INTEGRITY ARE ESSENTIAL FOR SALESPEOPLE IN TODAY'S BUSINESS LANDSCAPE."

Ethical selling practices are not just a set of rules to follow; they are the foundation of a successful and sustainable sales career. Upholding ethical principles, respecting the customer's decisions, and building a reputation for honesty and integrity are essential for salespeople in today's business landscape. Trust is the currency of sales, and ethical behaviour is the key to earning and maintaining that trust. In an age where social media can amplify both ethical successes and failures, ethical selling practices are more relevant than ever. By embracing ethics, salespeople can not only build prosperous careers but also contribute to a culture of integrity and trust within their organisations and the broader sales industry.

9.
SOCIAL SELLING AND NETWORKING

Social selling and networking have emerged as indispensable tools for modern salespeople seeking to expand their reach and generate hot leads.

Leveraging social media platforms to connect with target audiences, building relationships, establishing thought leadership, and utilising social media advertising are essential strategies for achieving these goals. This essay explores the importance of these practices in the context of modern sales, providing insights and actionable tips for sales professionals looking to maximise their impact in reaching a wider audience and filling their sales funnel with high-quality leads.

Leveraging Social Media Platforms to Connect with the Target Audience

A. The Digital Revolution in Sales

1. The Evolving Sales Landscape: The digital age has transformed the way customers engage with brands and make purchasing decisions. Salespeople must adapt to these changes.

2. The Role of Social Media: Social media platforms have become primary channels for customer engagement and brand interaction.

B. Identifying the Target Audience

1. Customer Profiling: Sales professionals should begin by creating detailed customer profiles to understand their target audience's demographics, preferences, and pain points.

2. Social Listening: Social media offers a wealth of data for understanding customer sentiment and preferences through social listening tools.

C. Building an Online Presence

1. Consistent Branding: Salespeople must maintain a consistent online presence across social media platforms, reflecting their personal brand and values.

2. Content Creation: Sharing valuable and relevant content establishes credibility and attracts the attention of the target audience.

Building Relationships and Establishing Thought Leadership

A. The Power of Relationship-Centric Sales

1. Shifting Focus: Modern sales are moving away from transactional approaches towards building meaningful, long-lasting relationships with customers.

2. Trust as the Foundation: Trust is the bedrock of any successful relationship. Salespeople must focus on building trust through their online interactions.

B. Engagement and Interaction

1. Active Engagement: Sales professionals should actively engage with their target audience by responding to comments, messages, and participating in discussions.

2. Providing Value: Sharing insights, knowledge, and expertise helps salespeople establish themselves as thought leaders in their industry.

C. Networking and Relationship Building

1. Connecting with Industry Peers: Building relationships with peers and industry influencers can open doors to new opportunities and collaborations.

2. Personalised Outreach: Salespeople should take a personalised approach to outreach, tailoring their messages to specific individuals or accounts.

Utilising Social Media Advertising to Reach a Wider Audience

A. The Potential of Social Media Advertising

1. The Reach of Social Platforms: Social media platforms offer powerful advertising capabilities, allowing salespeople to reach a broader audience than ever before.

2. Targeted Advertising: Social media advertising allows for precise targeting based on demographics, interests, and behaviours.

B. Creating Effective Social Media Ads

1. Compelling Visuals: Eye-catching visuals and multimedia content are essential to capture the audience's attention.

2. Persuasive Copywriting: Crafting persuasive and concise ad copy is crucial for conveying the message effectively.

C. Leveraging Paid Social Media Campaigns

1. Sponsored Content: Salespeople can promote their content to reach a larger, targeted audience.

2. Lead Generation Forms: Social platforms offer lead generation forms within ads, making it easier to collect valuable contact information from interested prospects.

The Importance of Analytics and Measurement

A. Tracking Performance

1. Analytics Tools: Utilising analytics tools provided by social media platforms allows salespeople to track the performance of their content and ads.

2. Data-Driven Decisions: Analysing data helps sales professionals understand what's working and what needs improvement in their social selling and networking efforts.

B. A/B Testing

1. Experimentation: A/B testing enables salespeople to experiment with different ad elements, such as headlines, visuals, and targeting criteria, to optimise campaign performance.

2. Continuous Improvement: Regularly reviewing and adjusting campaigns based on data insights is essential for maximising ROI.

While social selling and networking offer significant benefits, salespeople must also navigate challenges and avoid common pitfalls.

A. Time Management: Maintaining a strong online presence and engaging with a broader audience can be time-consuming. Sales professionals must strike a balance between their online and offline activities.

B. Authenticity: Authenticity is paramount in social selling. Salespeople must avoid coming across as insincere or overly promotional.

C. Privacy and Data Security: Salespeople must prioritise the privacy and data security of their connections and customers, adhering to relevant regulations.

"THROUGH SOCIAL MEDIA, SALESPEOPLE CAN EXPAND THEIR REACH AND FILL THEIR SALES FUNNEL WITH HIGH-QUALITY LEADS."

In the digital age, social selling and networking have become indispensable strategies for modern sales professionals aiming to reach a wider audience and generate hot leads. By leveraging social media platforms to connect with their target audience, building relationships, establishing thought leadership, and utilising social media advertising, salespeople can expand their reach and fill their sales funnel with high-quality leads. These practices not only align with the evolving sales landscape but also offer opportunities for building long-lasting customer relationships and staying ahead of the competition. While challenges exist, sales professionals who embrace social selling and networking will find themselves better equipped to thrive in the modern world of sales, where the power of digital connections can significantly impact their success.

10.

DATA-DRIVEN SELLING AND INSIGHTS

D ata has emerged as a powerful ally for salespeople seeking to stay ahead of the curve and make informed decisions. Data-driven selling and insights offer a transformative approach that enables sales professionals to collect, analyse, and utilise data from sales interactions and customer feedback to improve their strategies. We will now explore the paramount importance of data-driven selling, including the collection and analysis of data, identifying trends and patterns, and using data to personalise and optimise customer experiences. By harnessing the power of data, modern salespeople can unlock new levels of success and provide exceptional value to their customers.

Collecting and Analysing Data from Sales Interactions and Customer Feedback

A. The Data Revolution in Sales

1. The Rise of Big Data: Advances in technology have led to an explosion of data, providing sales professionals with a wealth of information to work with.

2. Real-Time Insights: Modern sales tools and platforms enable real-time data collection, making it possible to gather information from every customer interaction.

B. Sources of Data

1. Sales Interactions: Data can be collected from sales calls, emails, meetings, and other touch points between salespeople and customers.

2. Customer Feedback: Feedback channels, such as surveys, reviews, and social media, provide valuable insights into customer preferences and satisfaction.

C. Customer Relationship Management (CRM) Systems

1. CRM Benefits: CRM systems are essential tools for collecting, organising, and analysing customer data, helping salespeople track interactions and manage relationships.

2. Integrating Data: CRM systems allow for the integration of data from various sources, creating a comprehensive view of each customer's journey.

Identifying Trends and Patterns to Improve Sales Strategies

A. Data Analysis Techniques

1. Data Mining: Data mining involves extracting patterns and insights from large datasets to identify customer behaviours and preferences.

2. Predictive Analytics: Predictive analytics uses historical data to forecast future trends, helping salespeople anticipate customer needs and make proactive decisions.

B. Optimising Sales Funnel

1. Conversion Rate Analysis: Salespeople can use data to identify bottlenecks in the sales funnel and take steps to optimise the conversion process.

2. Lead Scoring: Data-driven lead scoring helps sales teams prioritise leads based on their likelihood to convert, allowing for more efficient resource allocation.

C. Competitive Analysis

1. Tracking Competitors: Data-driven insights can help sales professionals monitor competitor activities and adjust their strategies accordingly.

2. Benchmarking: Benchmarking against industry standards and competitors' performance provides a basis for setting goals and measuring success.

Using Data to Personalise and Optimise Customer Experiences

A. Personalisation as a Competitive Advantage

1. The Importance of Personalisation: Personalised experiences make customers feel valued and understood, increasing the likelihood of conversion and retention.

2. Tailoring Communication: Data-driven insights enable salespeople to tailor their communication and recommendations to individual customer preferences.

B. Customer Segmentation

1. Segmenting the Customer Base: Salespeople can use data to divide their customer base into distinct segments based on demographics, behaviour, or other factors.

2. Targeted Messaging: Each customer segment can receive targeted messaging and offers that resonate with their specific needs and interests.

C. Predictive Recommendations

1. Cross-Selling and Upselling: Predictive analytics can suggest complementary products or services to customers, increasing sales opportunities.

2. Product Recommendations: Data-driven algorithms can recommend products or solutions based on a customer's previous interactions and preferences.

The Ethical Considerations of Data-Driven Selling

A. Privacy and Data Protection

1. Respecting Customer Privacy: Sales professionals must ensure compliance with data protection regulations and respect customer privacy.

2. Transparency: Transparency in data collection and usage builds trust with customers and helps maintain ethical standards.

B. Avoiding Manipulation

1. Ethical Marketing: Salespeople should use data responsibly, avoiding manipulation or exploitation of customer information for personal gain.

2. Informed Consent: Customers should be fully informed about how their data will be used and have the option to opt out of data collection.

A. AI and Machine Learning

1. AI-Powered Sales Tools: AI and machine learning enable automation and data analysis, improving the efficiency of sales processes.

2. Sales Predictions: AI can generate accurate sales predictions, helping salespeople allocate resources more effectively.

B. Integrating Sales and Marketing

1. Aligning Efforts: Sales and marketing teams can collaborate by sharing data and insights, ensuring a unified approach to customer engagement.

2. Marketing Automation: Automation tools can deliver personalised marketing campaigns based on customer behaviour and interactions.

Challenges and Pitfalls in Data-Driven Selling

While data-driven selling offers significant advantages, salespeople must also navigate potential challenges and pitfalls.

A. Data Quality: Poor-quality data can lead to inaccurate insights and decisions. Sales professionals must ensure data accuracy and cleanliness.

B. Information Overload: The abundance of data can be overwhelming. Salespeople must focus on relevant metrics and insights to avoid information overload.

C. Balancing Automation and Personalisation: Striking the right balance between automation and personalised interactions is essential to avoid coming across as impersonal.

"DATA IS NOT JUST INFORMATION; IT IS THE KEY TO UNLOCKING THE FUTURE OF SALES"

The modern sales landscape, data-driven selling and insights have become indispensable tools for sales professionals seeking to expand their reach, generate hot leads, and provide exceptional customer experiences. By collecting and analysing data from sales interactions and customer feedback, identifying trends and patterns, and using data to personalise and optimise customer experiences, salespeople can unlock new levels of success and deliver unparalleled value to their customers. While challenges exist, those who embrace data-driven selling as an integral part of their sales strategy will find themselves better equipped to thrive in today's data-rich and highly competitive business environment. Data is not just information; it is the key to unlocking the future of sales.

11.

TECHNOLOGICAL AIDS TO SELLING

The sales landscape is constantly evolving, shaped by the rapid advancement of technology. In both Business-to-Business (B2B) and Business-to-Consumer (B2C) environments, sales professionals face the challenge of meeting increased targets with efficiency and precision. Sales automation and technology emerge as pivotal tools in this context, offering a pathway to streamline processes, manage customer data effectively, and enhance communication. This chapter explores how a salesperson can leverage these tools to excel in the contemporary sales environment.

Utilising Sales Automation Tools to Streamline Processes

Sales automation involves the use of software and tools to automate repetitive and time-consuming tasks in the sales process. Here's how it can be used effectively:

1. Automated Lead Generation and Nurturing: In both B2B and B2C settings, generating and nurturing leads is crucial. Automation tools can capture leads from various sources and nurture them with personalised email campaigns, increasing the chances of conversion.

2. Efficient Task Management: Sales automation tools can schedule appointments, set reminders, and follow-up emails. This automation saves significant time, allowing sales professionals to focus on more strategic tasks.

3. Enhanced Sales Pipeline Management: These tools help in tracking the progress of prospects through the sales funnel. Automated alerts can notify when a prospect moves to a new stage, enabling timely interventions.

Leveraging CRM Systems for Effective Customer Data Management

Customer Relationship Management (CRM) systems are integral for managing customer interactions and data:

1. Centralised Customer Information: In both B2B and B2C sales, having detailed customer information is vital. CRM systems provide a centralised database for all customer interactions, purchases, and preferences, which is crucial for personalised communication.

2. Tracking Sales Activities and Performance: CRM systems allow salespeople to track their activities, from calls made to emails sent, and analyse their performance against sales targets.

3. Predictive Analytics for Strategic Decisions: Advanced CRM systems use predictive analytics to forecast sales trends and customer behaviours, helping sales professionals in B2B and B2C to strategise effectively.

Effective communication and collaboration are key in sales:

1. Communication Tools for Client Engagement: Utilising tools like video conferencing and instant messaging can enhance interaction with clients, especially in B2B sales where building relationships is crucial.

2. Collaboration Tools for Team Coordination: In B2B environments, where sales cycles are longer and involve multiple stakeholders, collaboration tools help in coordinating efforts and sharing information seamlessly.

3. Mobile Technology for On-the-Go Access: Sales reps, especially in B2C, benefit from mobile technology that allows them to access customer data and sales tools anywhere, providing flexibility and improving responsiveness.

Application in B2B and B2C Sales Environments

The application of sales automation and technology varies in B2B and B2C environments:

1. B2B Sales: Here, the focus is on building long-term relationships. Automation can be used for personalised communication and nurturing high-value leads. CRM systems are crucial for managing complex customer data and long sales cycles.

2. B2C Sales: In B2C, the volume of transactions is higher, and decisions are made quicker. Automation in B2C focuses on efficiency in handling a large number of transactions and providing a personalised experience at scale.

For effective implementation, sales professionals should:

1. Understand the Customer Journey: Tailor automation tools to align with the customer's journey, ensuring that automation adds value at each stage.

2. Choose the Right Tools: Select tools that integrate well with existing systems and align with the specific needs of B2B or B2C sales.

3. Train and Adapt: Continuously train on new technologies and be adaptable to changes in the sales environment.

4. Monitor and Optimise: Regularly monitor the performance of automation tools and optimise them for better results.

"SALES AUTOMATION AND TECHNOLOGY ARE NOT JUST FACILITATORS BUT GAME-CHANGERS IN THE REALM OF SALES."

Sales automation and technology are not just facilitators but game-changers in the realm of sales. For sales professionals in both B2B and B2C environments, leveraging these tools can lead to unprecedented efficiency and effectiveness. The key lies in understanding the specific needs of their sales environment and implementing these technologies strategically. By doing so, salespersons can not only meet their targets with greater ease but also provide a more personalised and satisfying experience to their customers, thereby setting the stage for long-term success in the ever-evolving world of sales.

12.
TECHNOLOGICAL AIDS TO SELLING

The ability to continuously learn and upskill has become not just an advantage but a necessity. Whether one is engaged in Business-to-Business (B2B) or Business-to-Consumer (B2C) sales, the need to stay abreast of industry trends, develop new skills, and adapt to changing environments is critical. This essay explores the importance of continuous learning and up-skilling for sales professionals, focusing on staying up-to-date with industry trends, attending events and workshops, and engaging with sales communities and mentors.

Staying Up-to-Date on Industry Trends and Developments

The landscape of sales, influenced by technological advancements and changing consumer behaviours, is in constant flux. For sales professionals in both B2B and B2C sectors, understanding and adapting to these changes is vital.

1. Adapting to Market Changes: Sales professionals must be aware of emerging market trends, changes in consumer preferences, and new technological tools. This awareness allows them to adapt their sales strategies to remain competitive.

2. Leveraging Technological Advancements: Technologies such as CRM systems, AI, and data analytics are reshaping sales. Continuous learning in these areas can enhance efficiency and effectiveness.

3. Understanding Regulatory Changes: Especially in B2B sales, staying informed about regulatory changes in various industries can impact sales strategies and compliance.

Attending Industry Events, Workshops, and Webinars

Participating in industry events, workshops, and webinars is a practical way for sales professionals to gain insights and knowledge.

1. Networking Opportunities: These events provide platforms to connect with peers, industry leaders, and potential clients. Networking can lead to new business opportunities and partnerships.

2. Learning from Experts: Workshops and webinars often feature experts who share valuable insights and best practices. This exposure can provide sales professionals with new perspectives and strategies.

3. Skill Development: Many of these events offer training sessions that help sales professionals develop new skills, from negotiation tactics to using the latest sales software.

Engaging with Sales Communities and Mentors

Interaction with sales communities and mentors provides opportunities for growth, guidance, and support.

1. Learning from Peers: Engaging with sales communities, whether online or in person, allows sales professionals to learn from the experiences and challenges of their peers.

2. Mentorship: Having a mentor in the sales field can provide personalised guidance, career advice, and insights drawn from years of experience.

3. Staying Motivated: Being part of a community helps in maintaining motivation and enthusiasm, especially in the face of challenges and setbacks.

Application in B2B and B2C Sales Environments

The approach to continuous learning and up-skilling varies in B2B and B2C sales:

1. B2B Sales: Here, the focus is often on understanding complex products or services, long sales cycles, and building relationships with key decision-makers. Up-skilling in areas such as strategic account management, industry-specific knowledge, and consultative selling is crucial.

2. B2C Sales: In B2C sales, professionals need to excel in customer engagement, understanding consumer behaviour, and leveraging digital sales channels. Skills in social media marketing, customer experience management, and data analytics are highly beneficial.

Best Practices for Continuous Learning and Up-skilling

To effectively incorporate continuous learning into a sales career, professionals should:

1. Set Learning Goals: Identify specific areas for development and set achievable learning goals.

2. Allocate Time Regularly: Dedicate regular time for learning activities, whether it's reading industry publications, attending workshops, or engaging in online courses.

3. Apply Learning: Put new knowledge and skills into practice. This practical application reinforces learning and can lead to improved sales performance.

4. Share Knowledge: Sharing insights and knowledge with colleagues and peers not only reinforces one's own learning but also contributes to the development of others.

"SALES AUTOMATION AND TECHNOLOGY ARE NOT JUST FACILITATORS BUT GAME-CHANGERS IN THE REALM OF SALES."

Continuous learning and up-skilling are indispensable for any sales professional seeking long-term success in both B2B and B2C environments. The landscape of sales is characterised by rapid changes and intense competition. Those who commit to ongoing personal and professional development are better equipped to adapt, innovate, and excel. By staying up-to-date with industry trends, actively participating in learning events, and engaging with communities and mentors, sales professionals can enhance their skills, broaden their perspectives, and pave the way for a thriving career in sales. As the saying goes, "Learning is not a destination, but a journey," and this is especially true in the world of sales.

ABOUT THE AUTHOR

Pep McStone is a distinguished name in the realm of sales training, boasting an illustrious career that spans over two decades. With his extensive experience in sales training across various countries and industries, both in B2B and B2C sectors, McStone has established himself as a luminary in the field. His journey in sales training began in the bustling markets of Europe, where he honed his skills and developed a keen understanding of diverse sales dynamics in banking, finance, telecoms and business services. His expertise grew as he navigated through different cultural landscapes, from the fast-paced business hubs of Asia to the competitive markets of North America.

McStone's approach to sales is both holistic and pragmatic, blending traditional methods with innovative strategies. He is renowned for his ability to adapt sales techniques to suit different industries and personal styles of sales people, whether it's the high-stakes environment of tech sales or the nuanced world of consumer goods. This versatility has earned him accolades and a reputation as a sales mentor who can transform struggling sales teams into high performers.

A lifelong learner, McStone has continually evolved his methods to incorporate the latest in sales technology and psychology. His training sessions are a blend of engaging storytelling, practical insights, and actionable strategies, making him a sought-after speaker and trainer in international sales conferences.

In addition to his training endeavours, McStone is a prolific writer and thought leader in the sales and business community. His insights are regularly featured in leading sales and business publications, where he discusses the ever-changing landscape of sales and the importance of adaptability and continuous learning.

His book, distilled from his rich experience in diverse markets, is not just a testament to his sales expertise but also a guide for sales professionals aspiring to excel in their careers. McStone's narrative is not just about techniques and strategies; it's a journey through the various facets of sales, offering wisdom gleaned from his expansive career.

www.ingramcontent.com/pod-product-compliance
Lightning Source LLC
Chambersburg PA
CBHW071059290526
45795CB00004B/1562